Donald H. Richardson, Jr.

one

big

poem

Chestnut Hills Press

2006

one big poem

Chestnut Hills Press
306 Suffolk Road
Baltimore, Maryland
21218 USA

Book design by
Carmen M. Walsh
www.walshwriting.com

Author photo by
Carrie Mohoric

Distribution by
ItascaBooks
www.itascabooks.com

ISBN 978-0-932616-86-9

Printed in the United States of America

This one is for Clarinda,

who has since 1977 helped me in so many ways to keep going,
pointed me to my first teaching job,
published my first two poetry collections 》
which made it possible for me to work
with the Maryland State Arts Council
as a Poet in the Schools,
and made this new book possible.

》 **Books published through New Poets Series**

1982 *Knocking Them Dead*

1987 *Ghosts of Love*

acknowledgments

The following poems were previously published:

In *Maryland Poetry Review*

- ⟩ "The Year JFK Died (Windream)"
  [previously titled "The Year Kennedy Died"]
  Spring/Summer 1990

- ⟩ "Tropical Storm Danielle"
  Spring/Summer 1993

- ⟩ "A Long and Happy Life"
  [revised for this publication]
  Spring/Summer 1994

In *I Am: Self Portraits*
(a 1990 Dundalk Community College publication)

- ⟩ "Borrowing Sight"

- ⟩ "Survive"

contents

⟩

night

waters

The Great Love Affair (Maiden Voyage)

The street lunatic we passed
on the way to the dock
was yelling quietly to himself
then to someone in the dark
that it was too cold for swimming
winter was still there
and she smiled coldly at him
from deep in the night.

Later we heard
the sound of the ship
slapping the black water back
with us up above
the big name and the waterline
that crazy voice gone
deep behind us
our wake trailing back and back
to England.

Out on the ocean
the moon makes the water white
and the night
we are driving hard into
is broken now
by ghost-white islands
of floating ice
like the pieces
of a puzzle
with no picture at all.

Listen to the sea
as it hisses by
as it wishes us good-by
when we have passed
it will say this same thing
and we will be all

we ever dreamed of
and all they ever found.

But I wish to see you again
and this great love
that has gone but will not end
tonight will not end
this ship will not sink
and it cannot move fast enough
none of them can
tonight you know
it is much too cold for swimming
we would be crazy to try.

O Dear, and you so perfect and all
your smile so cold
last night and the great shining ship
the huge hole ripped in the heart of it
we can jump
but we can't survive.

But if you must swim on a night like this
wait for another moon-white island of ice
to float by
kiss her good-by
and swim for it.

If it's not too far
you might be all right
there will be other ships
and street lunatics
women and bright nights you might remember.

Greater pieces of ice when this one melts
and somewhere deeper down south
much warmer women
with great big hearts
that melt all night.

The Sea of Death

We will die now you and I
with the sea spread out
below the grey sky
caught ragged as a winter day
begging to be led away
there was blood on the trail today
thicker than the water they used
to wash it away.

The Sea of Life

Jump in to forget
who you are
who you ever were
pout your heart out
in the corner of some sad café
go west to forget
how you are always hornier
in California.

The Sea of Hate

Sometimes you can hate
everything you love
the sky below the sea above
when the waves turn you around
and around
then hold you down
till you cry
and wish your uncle would die.

The Sea of Love

I think it was the sea of love
we saw
that June day in Newport
after Tatsie died
the sea had come
her small waves barely breaking
out on the rocks
so blue so soft, so soft
to tell someone...

Night Waters

Summer nights fall
slowly into the water.
In the dark,
she kneels near the end of the dock
reaches into the night water
and touches the dark shape
of the fish in the moonlight.

Caught in the air
in her open hand
it flies out into the sky
filled with black water.
She sees a flash of white
and looks after it.

Hands caught together
she reaches deeper water
her dark shape turns
and flashes white once
meeting moonlight
out past the dock
the water ripples
in one small place.

Walking back to the house alone
she knows she can be caught
and go back.
Out there she touches carefully
all the shapes
that come so quickly in the dark.

Near Death

"No one suspects the days to be gods."
Emerson ☽

Leaning over from her knees
tending the grave of her young husband
an old woman with flowers finds death
has no companions.
She is both old and young at once
in his soft arms
she turns to bones and leaves the flowers
near death she suspects
the days are going somewhere
not too far from here
there are more flowers, more days
she leaves the flowers
and goes away with him
his heart so full with her once
an empty place for flowers now.

Tropical Storm Danielle

The storm is spreading now
Across Kent Island
Only 10 miles from here.

Bobby called from Tennessee to say
That Kenny died today,
Our childhood friend.

The summer of '62 is over
It's fall and 30 years are gone.
That night the storm turned northwest.

Please take care of us
So we aren't afraid,

There's just not much time
And the wind blows hard
We know about that.

But if there is some deep
Lack of love for us
Maybe we find what is enough.

I didn't go to Kenny's funeral
I thought of Bobby there
But what could I say?

Our old friend dead
And too young
I guess.

The storm did little damage here
But the wind kept me awake last night
Knowing it could have been much worse.

Hands

Now it's time to go
to move from mist and cold
and elements that hold you here
let go the ice in your hands
hold invisible hands

Let go the cold
waves of cold communication
stark dreams of space
and dead souls falling
through frightening air

The ice is breaking
thin as air above
suicide water
tides to nowhere are
waiting below

Suicides and tides
answer to no one
It always is now or never
and nothing you ever saw
comes back to tell you

Where it all went
in between a warm green blur and hard black
the fires are frozen and
nothing hurts so much
as this time gone

The tides come fast and hard
today you cannot understand
as hard as stone
then soft as love left
where you cannot touch it again

Out in the dark
the world disappears
into invisible hands
huge and filled with stars
your hands were there

Above the cold and ice
So close and I held on again and again.

The Year JFK Died (Windream)

The late November wind shoots past
then comes back fast
picking up all the leaves
surrounds the house and rushes
all the last leaves to sea
and turns my heart around.

It's almost 45 years since
these four people died:
my mother, my best friend,
the first girl I ever loved
and President Kennedy.

So after the first death
there was a mother, a lover and a friend.

That death is not here anymore
now it is only the wind
and I'm not in the house at all
I'm out with the wind
with the wind in a dream
that holds death within
and you see where you are
but the people you see can't get in
then they all get lost and you dream your way back
then you are fast awake.

My uncle told me about a dream he had
about his friend Jack Kennedy
and how he was trying in the dream to tell him
how the world had been since he died.

I would tell him the world has been
like a dream of wind
where only the wind has been.

Borrowing Sight

Sometimes I just sneak
through these days on borrowed time
and borrow faces
to explain why I am not with you.

We borrow so many things
places we are going
places where we have been
lawnmowers and lives.

I wanted to borrow
this blind girl's eyes
today I watched her
talking on the phone
her dog as usual waiting
maybe she was thinking,
"Why are you staring at me?"

I want to see you
the way you see me.

))

the

invisible

world

Survive

I'm not so much afraid
of death, I just
don't want to
get left
there.

White

A girl I knew lay in the church
in her open coffin
white as heaven waiting
white as 18 years gone
to the clouds
in the sky that summer day
white as the doctors and the nurses
in the hospital in 1962
after the accident
white as the wings of an angel
not there that day.

Airs

Instead of dressing
he put on airs
and went out into his world,
to see where he was to go
and what he was to do there.

Long Asleep

Long asleep in their deep beds
my grandparents never wake
when I sneak into their room
always trying to be so quiet.
So many nights I go there,
it is always summer
the shades wave gently,
I always hear them
tapping so softly to me
something, everything
from out there
in the dark air
that breathes into
their silent room.

A Long and Happy Life

Standing in a dry yellow field late fall
I think of you all who wished me well
as seasons all softly fading into one.
My heart goes out into this afternoon
floats above in all the blue
sails with dust rising from the road
wants to fly past all of this
because I know how

We just get deeper and deeper
into what is
until we become what isn't

The bright sky floats away into night
the yellow field turns white
moonlight dreams down the road

and I remember how
you wished me a long and happy life.
I follow the light till the moon is gone
and then I go
deeper and deeper into this season
isn't that where I'm supposed to go
with my heart and all
wasn't that what you told me?
But I want to stay here and remember how

You just got deeper and deeper
into what was
until you became what wasn't

Where else is there to go
is always the question
can there be a different road past this field,
and the season,
another afternoon, another night, another light
to reflect from some new moon
and where can I find you to help me see how?

I just get deeper and deeper
into what is
until I become what isn't

Christina 2006

She still shines
through all those summers
and lights the lives
we had then
like the most beautiful sunny day
there ever was
and every one was
when she was there with us.

Moon Over My Mammy

I want to hold the moon
but only for a moment
the moon over my mammy
who is dead and under
south of here.
Her death was gruesome
I guess
she burned up in fires
she could not put out
with all the gin...
She didn't stop
she got so some one could not
tell her how to stick around
so damn melo dram astic.
Now the moon has gone
where she went
I don't know but
she went there faster
than you can say
Disaster.

All the Difference

I once got lost out in the snow
the roads were froze
the woods were too
and then my nose
which I couldn't see because
it was snowing so hard
up the road and down the road
between the road and woods
where no road was,
and I wondered
was there ever a choice
or did we just go
the way we went
as carefully blind as the snow?

Maybe there were two roads
in the frozen wood
maybe more
I couldn't see
I didn't care
I took the one
that wasn't there.

Housework

O, Mother, do you feel the wind
deep as you are
in the home you now keep
does it sweep you off your feet
does it clean the place
where you have gone?
And where have you gone, Mommy,
deep to sleep?
Does the wind dust
where you never dusted?
The west wind would take
your hair somewhere
the wind from the east
you probably like the least
on your thin white feet.
Where does the wind find you
always busy somewhere else
with someone I never knew?

With You

I have thought of all the wind
and what it would do
and all the rain and the night
after you died
and there was no way
to take care of you.

I thought of all the earth
and you there
and a little more distant
from these stars tonight.
I thought to the clouds in the wind

if it does rain tomorrow
as it might
you will feel no rain... I don't know,

But I will put on my raincoat, a hat
and go watch the rain fall
and try to watch it all fall
down to you.

You must be nothing but bones now
I will try to share the rain with you
I will contend with the wind
it is cold and the night
I don't know it from the light
that much I share with you.

The Afternoon Moon

What is the moon going to do
Caught up there
White as a cloud in all that blue
I thought it was a cloud
Then I thought what
Am I going to do
Without you
And I found I didn't know
The moon from a cloud
It seemed so out of place
And I did too
I didn't know where
To find you.

Coming Again

We've got to bear our gettings
forget our bearings
forget out begetters
and what they were wearing
get going again
not backwards now
get up, get out
run, run
and all I have done
and I have not
forgot you yet
nor will I;
forget me
yet
I still got the blues
all sad Sunday night
all afternoon
my feet in my shoes
want to get out of here
but where?

Keeping People Alive

Sometimes it's hard
To keep all these people alive
The girl in black, the poet, the suicide,
Georgie who died that rough day in Annapolis
I saw him in the old hospital
Then watched the wind
Tear at the bay.
I read about the car crashes
The girl in white, the blonde, the summer end,
Eric with his guitar and his girlfriend,
Zandy who fell when I was away,
Tatsie with his seizures
Who is surely falling away,
Their mother in Virginia
Whose breath won't come,
Myself some days.

Monster

Sit inside the storm
sit here in the warm safe house
watch the sleet, the snow and rain
hear the wind out there wearing on and on
the monster is there.

The monster follows me everywhere
under the cold January rain
running down the far wet fields
bare trees, bare arms
stretch out through the dead days
as he runs and runs
and outruns each storm that comes.

Somewhere there is your bright heart
but out in the half dark
the monster waits
behind the dark days.

He was out there today
cold white teeth have dug in deep
across the snow wet ground
without a sound.

The monster follows awake or asleep
I don't know where he goes
but you know him like smoke
you haven't seen yet
and maybe you're scared to see how
entire afternoons just burned away.

I found him in a book
but he won't stay
he is out there again today
a long way out now across the snow wet fields

stronger than all the cold
that will never go away.

But sometimes I can see that summer
when I fell into your waiting heart
and it went on and on
and I wonder now
what heart is waiting
and what cold
what monster takes this day, this night
the brilliance and the silence
all the summers and the cold
you and your heart and your soul?

Dream World

Dreaming of worlds and how
there is always one to come
one to be in now
and one just gone
and everyone you know
will make them
as big as you want
or as small
touching you once in a while
then sometimes all at once
and then you understand
how the world is anything
and everything and everyone
you ever found waking up
within a world of dreams

Answers to Questions I Don't Know

Ask me all these questions
I do not know the answers to
all these answers I give to you
I don't know the questions to
you make me think so hard
I have to go back to before I remember
anything before I was
anything I can even remember
and you ask me when did my imagination start
I wonder when I started to imagine myself
as something I was not and maybe then
I can understand
and maybe that is not the answer
to why I do not believe in your God
or heaven or hell
or any gods or anything I cannot see
and often I do not believe in that
which I can or know the difference entirely
between chaos and design
of each day that is a gift
(from someone or something I can't or won't look at)
you open and look at it
in Time that schedules everything
or time out of my mind
that I make up and I am god of
or a clock that is on
the clockmaker gone
but every clock we can see is wrong
time is too fast or too slow
I wish you wouldn't ask me any more
answers to questions I don't know.

Old Detective Movie

These things have all been
here before
the hard cracked leather sofa
the wood hat rack in the corner
the long cheap desk
and out the one window
that black and white sky
a few clouds
we have all seen this old movie by now.

These days have all been
here before
people nobody knows anymore
hang their hats
sit on the sofa
sometimes lean on the long desk
look out the window at that sky
the same one we saw before.

These clues have all been
here before
no matter where we look for them
they come before us quietly
like the mystery always there
in those eyes staring
out the window at the sky
it takes time and thought to find
all these things that are missing.

These hours are so long we can lean on them
the sky has changed to night and rain
the office is empty
someone has gone to follow the clues
in an old hat pulled down
his eyes in shadows
in the dark behind the rain.

The Petrified Forest

Tough guys like you are easy to find
I can turn on the TV anytime and see
Bogart or someone shooting it out with the cops
the old gangster movies loaded with death
and blood dripping out of bullet holes
and ending in the dirt on the floor
the desert is dry
the gangsters never seem to get away.

Held up in a house beside the desert highway
that goes through the Petrified Forest
armed and surrounded, one cop dead
traffic stopped for miles and miles
the high power scopes focused
on what went wrong there today.

The second day of 1989
my son and I driving to Arizona
stuck in all this traffic
as someone tried all day to shoot it out alone
then turned the gun around.

So much of this seems artifice
and really useless
then it makes me nervous
but I'm not scared
not with my son.

I saw so many of the old movies
the dark cafes, the big old black cars
the tough guys talking tough
usually much too late at night
watching a kind of life and death game
of hide and seek
you never really want to play

and if you know too much
they won't let you get away.

Then you see how everything is connected
in some way and then you don't
want to play the game anymore.

Sitting in that traffic that day with him
thinking of all
the black and white focus of so many years gone away
thinking we'll never get out of here
thinking let me out of the car and I
will shoot it out with this guy
and when he's dead we can get away.

When the police dogs found the body
in the back of the small house
they let the traffic through and
we saw that place as we drove by
surrounded only by the desert now.

We didn't see the Petrified Forest
or any gangsters
but they were all around us
as we drove fast through the dark desert
that night.

Outlaw Archaeology

There are sharks
swimming around in my brain
all afternoon the South American sun
burns and burns us
the tip of one finger is numb
nothing is ever the same.

Someone is fooling around
with my bones
they know I was an outlaw
that's all I ever wanted to be
but it's over now
and they won't leave me alone.

It got pretty hot in Bolivia
didn't it, Kid?
too hot for us and what we did
then came the big showdown
South American gundown.

I can't feel my trigger finger
my teeth hurt and my head aches
I have a fever, my legs itch
I took everything I could
the money's gone and the love
what's there to be afraid of?

Go ahead and count the old bullet holes
think of us out there
with the hot lead coming
hot and scared and running for it.

Two February Days

Rosie talked last night
about the funeral on Saturday morning
she said how the wind had been blowing
the snow across the lady's grave
it was so cold out there.
She saw her friends sitting sadly
in the dark limousine
and remembered how strange it was
to see them just sitting there
with nothing else to do.
She asked me the date
as if she wanted to be sure
she told me how it had all happened years before
the same stupid church, the same cemetery, the same cold
they had even followed the same route in the snow
to put someone else in the ground
another old friend
and she couldn't remember exactly where
but she said it had been another cold
February like this one
and everything happening again
frightened her.
We had gone to Washington that afternoon
to a gallery and out to dinner
then driven back to Baltimore.
Out of the car we walked together in the cold wind
to a warm coffee bar
the windows were steamed up and
from outside everyone in there was a blur
inside her warm voice was sad
and close and remembering more
friendship and separation and her father's tears
she had not expected
her dear friend holding on to her
and both of them

crying so hard out there in the February cold
going through it all again.
It was hard to think about the cold ground out there
frozen now again
around that lady who had been
the mother all those years to Rosie's friends.

Last Family Trip 1961

I looked at those pictures
of our European trip
and didn't know who or what
to try to forget first
all over again
my sister that pretty girl
going off to school in Switzerland
my thin, tanned mother who was to die
in two years and me
the tan skinny 16-year-old kid
our young handsome father
who took us there
the big French ship
the brand new Jaguar
with all the luggage
that didn't fit

High As Jesus

(found poem)

Say
Turn back
The woods are...
Despite all you can do
It broke nimbly
High, flew
You saw
Offence
Seized
Evil
Truth, curse
No, yes and eased
More often.
No more though
Persuade, close.
Voluntarily I prosper my role
I give
Misfortune
Self-control
Chatter for peace
Concerning
Paul.
Instructions indeed
Written in Greece
High again
As Jesus.

selected

new

poems

2003–2006

A House Is Not a Home

It is a ship sailing to
"that region where the air is music"
(Emerson, Essays Second Series*)*
where everyone is. 🌙

Once we said a house is shelter
and so it is
shelter from the storm
this one or any one

And a home is made out of bones
final shelter and
none at all

A house does not stay where it is
but goes where each dream takes it
it sails out of this world
like some great ship
through the grass, the trees, the sky and the clouds
above all of it

It goes where all who lived there went
and finds them again and again
with sure navigation
across seas of love and hate
loss and gain
life and death
beyond anything that tries
to keep it where it is

You go out at night and throw the anchor out
with no line attached to it
you do not know the direction of time
you do not know where you live.

Writing in the Rain

That summer
we were sitting
at a table in the rain
under a tent
that the rain went right through
and a dime fell
and the dime falling
then spinning
on the wet glass of the table
sounded like the rain
falling

She and he and I
were sitting there
and he was writing
stories about the war
she was writing about someone
who wasn't there
on cold wet paper

I was the one who let the dime fall
and asked to borrow her pen
to write about how these things
never change

Of course
I was in love with her
and began to write
the Question
to send her:
will you love me now and
then the answer was falling
all over everything
like the rain

And we could not turn away
from this dream
like some old movie
that sounded like the rain
falling on wet glass
like her laugh
when she said
yes,
love is like this rain
falling all summer

And then it was always
raining again
and my dime fell down
into the empty phone
and no one called back

and all summer we sat
at that table in the rain
and wrote
on the cold wet glass
no one called
no one left
no one came
no one ever
felt that rain.

Balm

I remember as a child seeing
a mother pig and six baby pigs
suckling in the cold March mud
I was just waiting for spring
I knew then
we would all be warm again

Didn't you know
everything is a metaphor
for everything else

Yesterday
I passed this poor ragged lady
carrying her crazy things
in blue plastic bags
up our windy road
it was no dream

Then my father went by
complete
in his tailored English suit
with the sleeves too long
an impossible thing
except in my dream

Is there any balm
for anything?

February now
I got
the sun in my eyes
driving home straight
into it

And later
these cold ships on the water

just look mean
their gray winter hulls
anchored tonight
in winter moonlight
like unwanted dreams

Silent Movie

How the night just
comes and goes
like a muscle twitching
into the shape of things
that come to you
you don't know
like a silent movie
moving inside you

And why didn't I
trust in the death
and destruction of
those childhood dreams
why did I go on
believing in those things?

Waiting

I've been to heaven.
It was a waiting room
with soft stuffed chairs
and tall windows with clouds to view.
On the sills and tables were magazines
all filled with nothing but good news.
You get to sit there and read them
whenever you want to.

Chinese Boxes

One inside another
each one smaller
and each one empty
like wishes
like prayers
they take so long
to open
to get to the last
the smallest
the most empty one
and there is god.

Tiger Shark

The tiger's talent
is deep and silent
under water never
still he comes for you
as the undertow
pulls you down
into the start
of his sharp rush
at your heart.

Wanting Pictures

(For Sarah)

Despondering my deep fate this late
you will need search parties to found
where I have gone away too lone
I um fall flat and despare is where?
and ever since before
what has happen small and far
all the leaves rattling down
around here and no one to see that
I have press the button marked depress
behind the glass full and dark and
cruel hard whirl goes curling
round my dreams and days and telephones
ring tight around my heart
which is often open
and wanting pictures to tell how much
more I love the world than this.

Jesus Was

Jesus was what
loves me this love
goes also by the name of Christ
who was born some long time ago.
They killed Jesus young
Romans or Jews or someone
He died for my sins
like ice melting
in my hands. But Christ
they told me
he was not cold for long
and then he was gone.
Was he in my back pocket
in my last drink
in what I always loved?
I think of him but
I have never seen him
I have never heard him.
They told me he had come and
in the heat and blinding light
Jesus was waiting for me
on a cross, on a mountain above
in a flood of all the love
I have ever known.
Spring rain
falling cold into a cold sea
someone waiting for me
Why do you go falling
falling into the sea, Jesus?
But wasn't Jesus walking above?
I never knew where he was.
Wherever I looked Jesus had
come to such pain
and was always dying young
just as spring came.

In This World

In this world
everything is hidden
and everything is clear
everything is far away
and everything is near.
A baby held above the flood,
a baby floating downstream,
the love of gods
no one has ever seen.

Easter 2002

Happy Easter,
Mister,
and don't forget
about that cross
all shaped like pain.
You won't see it
much at the mall
where giant rabbits deliver
the message shaped
like an egg.
We are all going to lie
some way.

It's Too Late to Say
Anything to Edna St. Vincent Millay

My life is just one big poem
a heart with feathers
wild and coole as a swan trailing
all the other swans
a tattered, ragged bony thing
singing like wild geese that say
everything is OK there is time
but there is no beach
no mermaids but each of us
may whisper to the waves
and listen:
one day in Paris I met
Edna St. Vincent Millay
she looked just great
beautiful as the snow.
It was winter 1928
she was shy and ran
off into the hemlocks
back in the snow
like a dear she knows
the way and what not to say
later there are scarlet begonias
and a sleek and silent water rat
and that lover I try to fit into
and everything that I want for
my life which is just this one big poem
with a thousand phantoms
passing like cars with big fins
slaves and savage ends
laundry and my soul located finally exactly
love calling too
and some of the strangest things
in the world depend upon
the tabloid I saw that told how it knew where

my soul was
and the wind only knows the words for these
tigers tearing through the ice cream
in the freezers of the night
emperors with the doors closed
the scholar singing in the rose-garden
all spread out against the English sky
let's go
but listen:
before you leave that garden
alive and singing
in the fog like stone and shaking
altered forever
she was screaming
give me some thing in return
I gave you everything there was
chew your gum
and you can count me in with all

these leaves flying past everything
maybe we will plunge into them
and learn them all
by heart, my heart,
because that's all that's left you now
all but this poem from a common spring
running six feet underground
this spring and all our small hands in the rain
holding handfuls of rain
fugitives from our future
and nothing can bring
back the power of the hungry heart
of an idle king
but hearts are lame with running after
hearts and hearts passing these visions
in the night sinking and fading
and just getting cold as dust and just
as old and sleeping, sleeping
and going home saying good-by to you

in this strange, strange language
you know the dead sands and blue latitudes
the sky where no sky is
the voice, the music whispered from the sea
to him and to you and to me
so this poem is such a cry
now listen:
to it all.

Christmas Picture

Maybe it was angels then
singing some sweet music
I heard it ringing
cold and white and lacing
out in the snow and wind
bringing Christmas morning
to us in that big house.
Later sitting on the back stairs
where my father would take our picture,
there were six of us grandchildren,
I sat on the stairs and put
my hands on my cousin's shoulders below
and my sister's hands on my shoulders from above
waiting for the picture,
presents, Christmas,
love.

Small Worlds

When you are only nine
you cannot resist the wish
to turn the world upside down,
so easy to hold it
the glass tight in your hands
so clear all around then
the white comes falling,
you want to see it always
cover everything
in that little world
of Christmas time.

Up Here

Up here
In this dream
the clouds
are in pieces.
I see them
again and again
like someone ripped them up
and threw them at me
duck!

What I Don't Want

I don't want to read
I don't want to write
I don't want to love
I don't want to fight
I don't want a push
I don't want a shove
I don't want to look
At the stars above
I don't want a dog
I don't want a cat
I don't want a bird
Or anything like that
I don't want a hug
I don't want a shrug
I don't want a ceiling
I don't want a rug
I don't want these walls
These halls or these rooms
I don't want what I got
I don't want what's not
I don't want to be cruel
I don't want to be kind
I don't want to seek
I don't want to find
I don't want to tell you
Any of this
It's all mine.

O These Leaps of Indifference

O these leaps
of indifference!
they take you
puddle jumping
muddling fuddling
faith always in
cows and moons
jumping, jumping
for joy, for joy
lately so coy
my silver spoon
always in my
open mouth

Chicago Dream

Someone asked me if I knew
why my mother died
I looked across Chicago
and couldn't see the other side
I didn't know anybody there
our train had just arrived
with this girl and her boyfriend
for some reason I was with them
it was almost morning that night
I dreamed this dim ride
Chicago looked so far and wide
I couldn't see the other side.
Someone turned the lights on
but it was dark outside
and I had no idea where to go
not knowing anyone there
not having planned this thing at all.

You Can Go Home Again

I wonder what it will be like
when I go home again
I know I can
I know where it is
and how to get there
after years and years
of here and there
what I know
and what I don't
telling everything
and telling nothing
saying the wrong things
and the right things
to everyone
and no one
some beauty
and all the rest of it
then home free at last
at best
a moment regained
for only a moment
what a goddamned paradise
never lost
never found.